JOHN MURPHY
on

Chart
Analysis

BY JOHN J. MURPHY

Includes **FREE** Bridge/CRB demo disk

TRADE SECRETS

John Murphy on Chart Analysis

JOHN J. MURPHY

This publication is designed to provide accurate and authoritative
information in regard to the subject matter covered. It is sold
with the understanding that neither the author nor the publisher
is engaged in rendering legal, accounting, or other professional
service. If legal advice or other expert assistance is required, the
services of a competent professional person should be sought.

*From a Declaration of Principles jointly adopted by a
Committee of the American Bar Association and a Committee
of Publishers.*

This book, along with other books, are available at
discounts that make it realistic to provide them as gifts
to your customers, clients, and staff. For more information on these long lasting, cost effective premiums,
please call John Boyer at 800.424.4550 or e-mail him at
john@traderslibrary.com.

ISBN 1-883272-29-7

Printed in the United States of America.

Contents

Introduction

A lot has happened in the world of technical analysis since this booklet was first published in 1989. That doesn't mean that the principles discussed herein aren't still valid. On the contrary, the technical principles explained in this booklet are as valid today as they were ten years ago. The changes have more to do with the broader application of technical analysis by professional traders and the investing public. With the growing use of personal computers, and ready access to the Internet, the ability to chart markets has increased dramatically. Charting software is relatively inexpensive. Many Internet services allow the public to chart for free. That increased access has contributed to a much greater use of charts for decision-making purposes, which has helped produce a much greater understanding and appreciation of what charts can do.

A second change has to do with a greater appreciation of the role of the futures markets. Ten years ago, this booklet might have been of interest only to futures traders. Today's stock trader knows, however, the trends in the futures markets have a tremendous influence on the stock market. Rising bond futures prices, for example, are generally positive for stock prices. Rising bond prices are caused by falling commodity futures prices, like gold and oil (which are reflected in a declining CRB Futures Price Index). One of the factors pushing commodity prices lower is a rising dollar futures contract. The relationship between the S&P 500 cash index and its related futures contract trigger program trading strategies, which can cause significant swings in the stock market on a day to day basis.

Even on a sector by sector basis, the futures markets can help determine stock market strategies. Falling commodity prices have a negative impact on stock groups tied to those commodities — like copper, gold, and energy shares. A strong Treasury bond market usually has a positive impact on interest rate-sensitive stock groups like banks, financials, and utilities. Given all of the linkages that exist between the stock market and the various futures markets, it's more important than ever to know how to follow trends in the futures pits — and that's where charts come into play.

The chart examples shown in this booklet are the same ones used in the original publication and are based on the futures markets. The basic concepts, however, shown on the charts are timeless. It's also good to know that the charting concepts described herein can be applied to all markets — including stock indexes, stock sectors, individual stocks and even mutual funds (as well as the futures markets themselves). One of the greatest benefits of technical analysis is its applicability to any and all markets.

Charts can be used in conjunction with economic and fundamental analysis. Charts can be used to help time entry and exit points in the implementation of fundamental strategies. Charts can also be used as an alerting device to warn the trader that something may be changing in a market's underlying fundamentals. Whichever way you choose to employ them, charts can be an extremely valuable tool — if you know how to use them. This booklet is a good place to start learning how.

John J. Murphy

JOHN MURPHY
on

Chart
Analysis

Chapter 1

WHY IS CHART ANALYSIS SO IMPORTANT?

Successful participation in the futures markets virtually demands some mastery of chart analysis. Consider the fact that all decisions in the futures markets are based, in one form or another, on a market forecast. Whether the market participant is a futures speculator, a hedger, an option trader or a spread trader, *price forecasting* is usually the first, most important step in the decision making process. To accomplish that task, there are two methods of forecasting available to the futures analyst — the fundamental and the technical.

Fundamental analysis is based on the traditional study of supply and demand factors that cause market prices to rise or fall. In the agricultural markets, for example, such factors as crop conditions and weather forecasts would be considered. In financial markets, the fundamentalist would look at such things as corporate earnings, trade deficits, and changes in the money supply. The intention of this approach is to arrive at an estimate of the intrinsic value of a futures market in order to determine if the market is over- or under- valued.

Technical or chart analysis, by contrast, is based on the study of the market action itself. While fundamental analysis studies the reasons or causes for prices going up or down, technical *analysis studies the effect, the price movement itself.* That's where the study of price charts comes in. Chart analysis is extremely useful in the price-forecasting process. Charting can be used by itself with no fundamental input, or in conjunction with fundamental information. Price forecasting, however, is only the first step in the decision-making process.

Market Timing

The second, and often the more difficult, step is *market timing*. Since commodity futures markets are so highly leveraged (initial margin requirements are generally less than 10% of a contract's value), minor price moves can have a dramatic impact on trading performance. Therefore, the precise timing of entry and exit points is an indispensable aspect of any market commitment. To put it bluntly, *timing is everything in the futures market*. For reasons that will soon become apparent, timing is almost purely technical in nature. This being the case, it can be seen that the application of charting principles becomes absolutely essential at some point in the decision-making process. Having established its value, let's take a look at charting theory itself.

Chapter 2

WHAT IS CHART ANALYSIS?

Chart analysis (also called *technical analysis*) is the study of market action, using price charts, to forecast future price direction. *The cornerstone of the technical philosophy is the belief that all of the factors that influence market price — fundamental information, political events, natural disasters, and psychological factors — are quickly discounted in market activity.* In other words, the impact of these external factors will quickly show up in some form of price movement, either up or down. *Chart analysis, therefore, is simply a shortcut form of fundamental analysis.*

Consider the following: A rising price reflects *bullish* fundamentals, where demand exceeds supply; falling prices would mean that supply exceeds demand, identifying a *bearish* fundamental situation. These shifts in the fundamental equation cause price changes, which are readily apparent on a price chart. The chartist is quickly able to profit from these price changes without necessarily knowing the specific reasons causing them. The chartist simply reasons that rising prices are indicative of a bullish fundamental situation and that falling prices reflect bearish fundamentals.

Another advantage of chart analysis is that the market price itself is usually a leading indicator of the known fundamentals. Chart action, therefore, can alert a fundamental analyst to the fact that something important is happening beneath the surface and encourage closer market analysis.

Charts Reveal Price Trends

Markets move in trends. The major value of price charts is that they reveal the existence of market trends and greatly facilitate the study of those trends. Most of the techniques used by chartists are for the purpose of identifying significant trends, to help determine the probable extent of those trends, and to identify as early as possible when they are changing direction. (See Figure 1.)

Types Of Charts Available

The most popular type of chart used by commodity futures analysts and traders is the *daily bar chart* (shown in Figure 1) provided by the *Bridge/CRB Futures Perspective*. Another popular type of chart is the *point and figure chart* (shown in Figure 2). Point and figure charting utilizes a series of X's and O's to record market movement and does not take time or volume into account. While that form of charting is beyond the scope of this discussion, suffice it to say that point and figure charts can be valuable when used in conjunction with bar charts.

Weekly and Monthly Bar Charts

While the bar chart is most commonly applied to *daily* price action, bar chart construction can be applied to *weekly* and *monthly* charts as well. These longer-range charts, going back as far as 20 years, provide an invaluable long-term perspective on market movement that is impossible to achieve with daily charts alone. (See Figures 22 & 23.)

Figure 1: The above chart of June Treasury Bonds is an excellent example of a market trend. Charts facilitate the study of trends. Important trends persist once they are established.

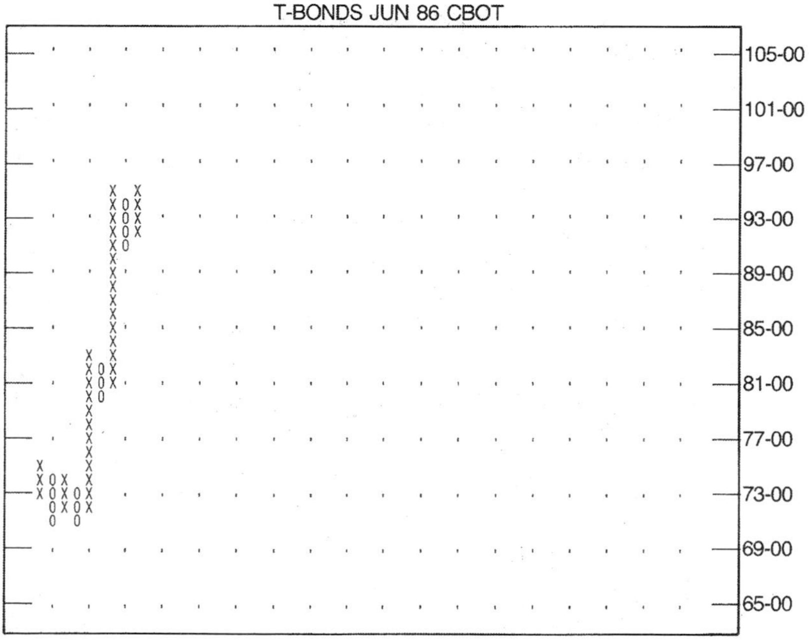

T-BONDS JUN 86 CBOT

Figure 2: A point and figure chart of the same uptrend shown in Figure 1. Prices are recorded with X's and O's.

Price, Volume and Open Interest

The daily bar chart (Figure 3) includes three essential pieces of market information. In addition to recording the price movement of the individual futures contract, volume and open interest are also included. These data enable the futures chartist to take a three-dimensional approach to market analysis, that is, to blend their relative impact in the analytical process.

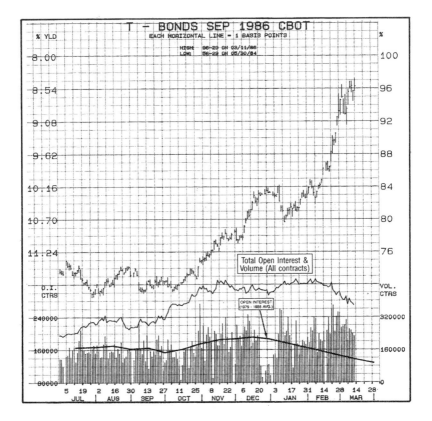

Figure 3. A daily chart with volume and open interest included. The vertical bars at the bottom of the chart show volume. The solid line near the bottom of the chart is the six-year average of open interest and is used to plot the seasonal tendency.

Chapter 3

HOW TO PLOT
THE DAILY BAR CHART

Price plotting is an extremely simple task. The daily bar chart has both a vertical and horizontal axis. The vertical axis (along the side of the chart) shows the price scale, while the horizontal axis (along the bottom of the chart) records calendar time. The first step in plotting a given day's price data is to locate the correct calendar day. This is accomplished simply by looking at the calendar dates along the bottom of the chart. Every five-day period (a trading week) is marked with a darker vertical grid to facilitate time comparisons and plotting. Plot the high low and closing (settlement) prices for the futures contract. A vertical bar connects the high and low (the range). The closing price is recorded with a horizontal tic to the right of the bar. (Some chartists mark the opening price with a tic to the left of the bar.) Each day simply move one step to the right.

Volume is recorded with a vertical bar along the bottom of the chart. *Open interest* is placed just over the volume bar and can be identified by a solid line. *Total volume* and open interest figures for each individual delivery month, the total figures (all contracts combined) are considered to be more useful in the forecasting process. Official volume and open interest figures are usually released the following day by the various exchanges. Therefore, there is a one-day lag in plotting those two figures. The solid line near the bottom of the chart is the 6-year average of open interest figures and is used to track the seasonal open interest tendency. (See section, "The Interpretation of Volume and Open Interest.")

It's not necessary for the user to construct the daily charts. *Bridge/CRB Futures Perspective* provides a fresh set of charts each week. Included with the price charts is an arsenal of technical information and indicators that aid in the analysis of the charts themselves. Technical comments are also provided, adding dimension and an independent perspective to the user's work.

Charts Are Used Primarily To Monitor Trends

Two basic premises of chart analysis are that *markets trend* and that *trends tend to persist.* Trend analysis is really what chart analysis is all about. Trends are characterized by a series of peaks and troughs. An *uptrend* is a series of rising peaks and troughs. A *downtrend* shows descending peaks and troughs. Finally, *trends* are usually classified into three categories: major, secondary, and minor. A *major* trend lasts more than six months; a *secondary* trend, from one to three months; and a *minor* trend, usually a couple of weeks or less.

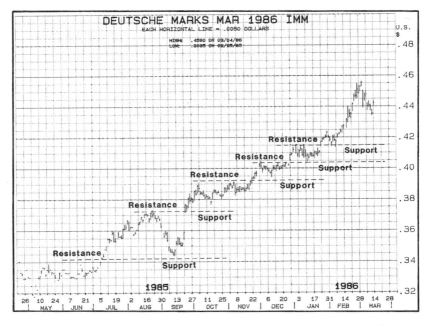

Figure 4: An uptrend is a series of rising peaks and troughs. The peaks represent resistance and the troughs show support. Notice that previous resistance peaks usually provide support once they are exceeded on the up side.

Chapter 4

SUPPORT AND RESISTANCE
TRENDLINES AND CHANNELS

There are two terms that define the peaks and troughs on the chart. A previous trough usually forms a support level. *Support* is a level *below the market* where buying pressure exceeds selling pressure and a decline is halted. *Resistance* is marked by a previous market peak. Resistance is a level *above the market* where selling pressure exceeds buying pressure and a rally is halted. (See Figures 4 & 5.)

Support and resistance levels reverse roles once they are distinctively broken. That is to say, a broken support level under the market becomes a resistance level above the market. A broken resistance level over the market functions as support below the market. The more recently the support or resistance level has been formed, the more power it exerts on subsequent market action. This is because many of the trades that helped form those support and resistance levels have not been liquidated and are more likely to influence future trading decisions.

The trendline is perhaps the simplest and most valuable tool available to the chartist. An up trendline is a straight line drawn up and to the right, connecting successive rising market bottoms. The line is drawn in such a way that all of the price action is above the trendline. A *down trendline* is drawn down and to the right, connecting the successive declining market highs. The line is drawn in such a way that all of the price action is below the trendline. An up trendline, for example, is drawn when at least two rising reaction lows (or troughs) are visible. However, while it takes two points to draw a trendline, *a third point is necessary to identify the line as a valid trend line.* If prices in an up trend dip back down to the trendline a third time and bounce off it, a valid up trendline is confirmed. (See Figures 6 & 7.)

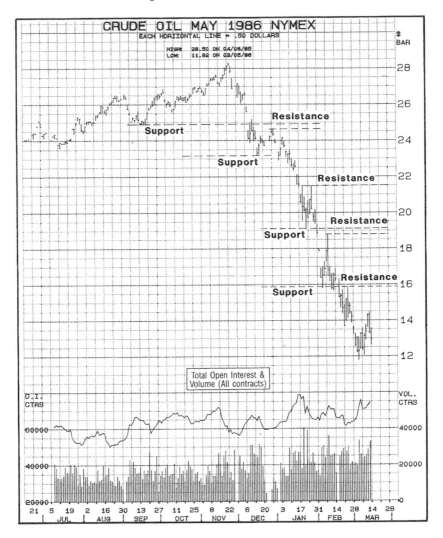

Figure 5: A *downtrend* is a series of descending peaks and troughs. Each peak is a *resistance* and each previous trough represents *support*. Once a support trough is broken on the downside, it usually provides resistance above the market on subsequent bounces.

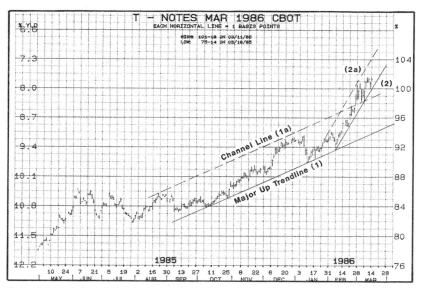

Figure 6: Line 1 shows a major *up trendline*. Notice that the line was touched four times during the uptrend. The "test" of the up trendline in January and February would have provided an excellent buying opportunity. Line 2 is a short-term up trendline. Lines 1a and 2a are examples of channel lines, drawn parallel to the up trendlines.

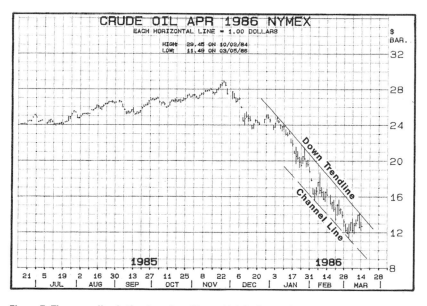

Figure 7: The upper line is the *down trendline*, which is drawn above rally peaks. The lower *channel line* is parallel to the upper line and often provides support during downtrends.

John Murphy on Chart Analysis   **11**

Trendlines have two major uses. They allow identification of support and resistance levels that can be used, while a market is trending, to initiate new positions. As a rule, the longer a trendline has been in effect and the more times it has been tested, the more significant it becomes. The violation of a trendline is often the best warning of a change in trend.

Channel lines are straight lines that are drawn parallel to basic trendlines. A rising channel line would be drawn above the price action and parallel to the basic trendline (which is below the price action). A declining channel line would be drawn below the price action and parallel to the down trendline (which is above the price action). Markets often trend within these channels. When this is the case, the chartist can use that knowledge to great advantage by knowing in advance where support and resistance are likely to function.

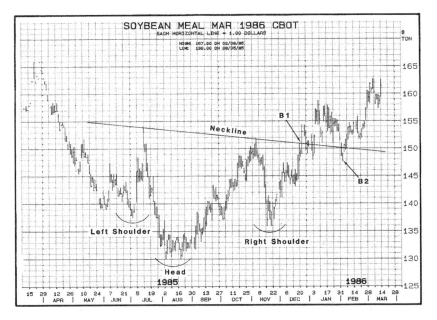

Figure 8: Example of a *head and shoulders* bottom. Notice the three prominent lows, with the middle trough (the head) lower than both the *shoulders*. The major buy signal is given where the *neckline* is broken on the upside (point B1). A *return move* back to the neckline (point B2) often provides a second chance to buy.

Chapter 5

REVERSAL AND CONTINUATION PRICE PATTERNS

One of the more useful features of chart analysis is the presence of price patterns, which can be classified into different categories and which have predictive value. These patterns reveal the ongoing struggle between the forces of supply and demand, as seen in the relationship between the various support and resistance levels, and allow the chart reader to gauge which side is winning. Price patterns are broken down into two groups — reversal and continuation patterns. *Reversal* patterns usually indicate that a trend reversal is taking place. *Continuation* patterns usually represent temporary pauses in the existing trend. *Continuation patterns take less time to form than reversal patterns and usually result in resumption of the original trend.*

Reversal Patterns: The Head And Shoulders

The *head and shoulders* is the best known and probably the most reliable of the reversal patterns. A head and shoulders top is characterized by three prominent market peaks. The middle peak, or the *head,* is higher than the two surrounding peaks (*the shoulders*). A trendline (*the neckline*) is drawn below the two intervening reaction lows. A close below the neckline completes the pattern and signals an important market reversal. (See Figure 8.)

Price objectives or targets can be determined by measuring the shapes of the various price patterns. The measuring technique in a topping pattern is to measure the vertical distance from the top of the head to the neckline and to project the distance downward from the point where the neckline is broken. The head and shoulders bottom is the same as the top except that it is turned upside down.

Double and Triple Tops and Bottoms

Another one of the reversal patterns, the *triple top or bottom*, is a variation of the head and shoulders. The only difference is that the three peaks or troughs in this pattern occur at about the same level. *Triple* tops or bottoms and the *head and shoulders* reversal pattern are interpreted in similar fashion and mean essentially the same thing. (Figure 9.)

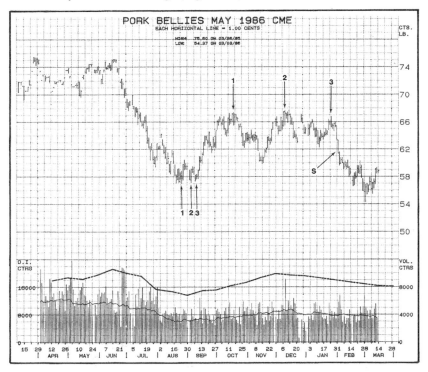

Figure 9: Example of *triple tops and bottoms*. The low in August shows three bottoms, forming a small *triple bottom*. The three peaks in October, December and January near 67 formed a more important *triple top* reversal pattern. The close below 62 gave an important sell signal (at S).

Double tops and bottoms (also called M's and W's because of their shape) show *two* prominent peaks or troughs instead of *three*. A *double top* is identified by two prominent peaks. The inability of the second peak to move above the first peak is the first sign of weakness. When prices then decline and move under the middle trough, the double top is completed. The measuring technique for the double top is also based on the height of the pattern. The height of the pattern is measured and projected downward from the point where the trough is broken. The double bottom is the image of the top. (See Figures 10 & 11.)

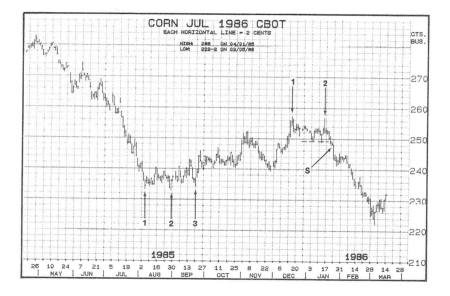

Figure 10: Examples of a *triple bottom* and a *double top*. Three low points in August and September formed a *triple bottom* and launched the rally. The top formed in December and January shows two prominent peaks at the same level, forming a *double top* reversal pattern. The close before support at 249 (point S) gave an important sell signal.

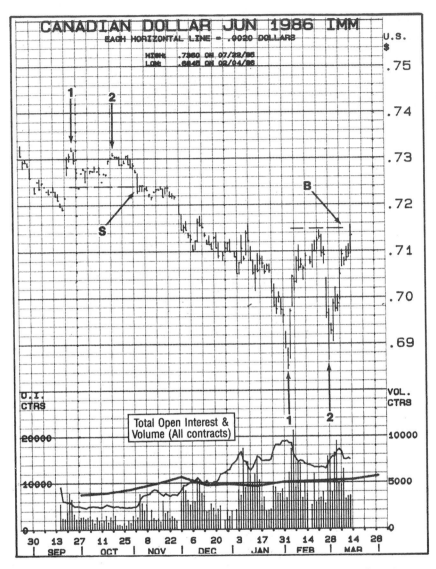

Figure 11: The top at the upper left is a *double top*. A profitable sell signal was given at point S. The two prominent lows formed in February may be a *double bottom*. A buy signal would be given at point B if the February peak is overcome.

Saucers and Spikes

These two patterns aren't as common, but are seen enough to warrant discussion. The *spike* top (also called a V-reversal) pictures a sudden change in trend. What distinguishes the *spike* from the other reversal patterns is the absence of a transition period, which is sideways price action on the chart constituting topping or bottoming activity. This type of pattern marks a dramatic change in trend with little or no warning. (Figure 12.)

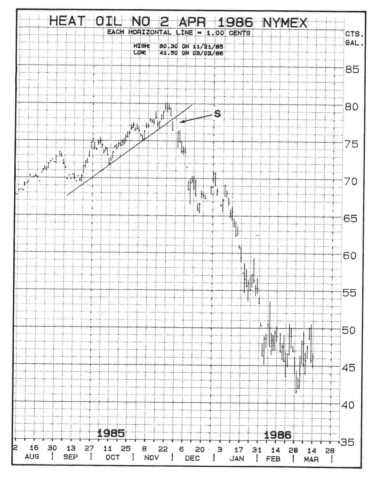

Figure 12: The petroleum markets are notorious for forming *spike tops and bottoms. Spike* reversals picture sudden changes in trend with little or no warning. Often the signal is the breaking of a tight trendline as at point S, where a sell signal was given.

The saucer, by contrast, reveals an unusually slow shift in trend. Most often seen at bottoms, the saucer pattern represents a slow and more gradual change in trend from down to up. The chart picture resembles a saucer or rounding bottom (hence its name). (Figure 13.)

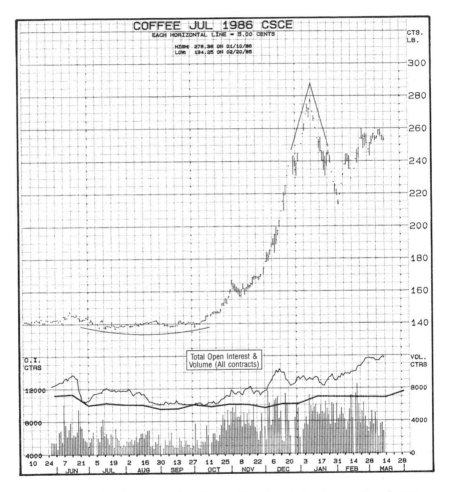

Figure 13: Examples of a *saucer bottom* (lower left) and a *spike* (or V-reversal) top (upper right). The *saucer* bottom is a slow and gradual process. The *spike* top is an abrupt turn to the downside (resembling an inverted V).

Continuation Patterns: Triangles

Instead of warning of market reversals, continuation patterns are usually resolved in the direction of the original trend. Triangles are among the most reliable of the continuation patterns. There are three types of triangles that have forecasting value — symmetrical, ascending and descending triangles. Although these patterns sometimes mark price reversals, they usually just represent pauses in the prevailing trend.

The *symmetrical triangle* (also called the *coil*) is distinguished by sideways activity with prices fluctuating between two converging trendlines. The upper line is declining and the lower line is rising. Such a pattern describes a situation where buying and selling pressure are in balance. Somewhere between the halfway and the three-quarters point in the pattern, measured in calendar time from the left of the pattern to the point where the two lines meet at the right (the *apex*), the pattern should be resolved by a breakout. In other words, prices will close beyond one of the two converging trendlines. (Figure 14.)

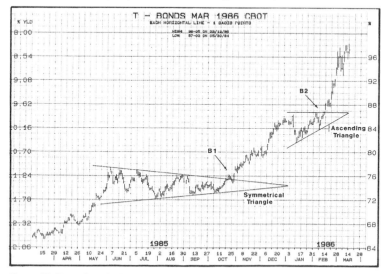

Figure 14: Examples of *triangles*. The *symmetrical triangle* to the lower left shows two converging trendlines, with the upper line descending and the lower line rising. It is usually a continuation pattern. The upside breakout at B1 completed the pattern and gave an excellent buy signal. The *ascending triangle* to the upper right shows a flat upper line and a rising lower line. It is usually a bullish pattern. The buy signal was given at B2.

The *ascending triangle* has a flat upper line and a rising lower line. Since buyers are more aggressive than sellers, this is usually a bullish pattern.

The *descending triangle* has a declining upper line and a flat lower line. Since sellers are more aggressive than buyers, this is usually a bearish pattern. (Figure 15.)

Figure 15: Example of a *descending triangle*. This pattern shows a descending upper line and a flat lower line. It is usually a bearish pattern. The lower line was broken and a sell signal given at point S. The subsequent rally in January failed to break through the overhead resistance formed by the *triangle*.

The measuring technique for all three triangles is the same. Measure the height of the triangle at the widest point to the left of the pattern and measure that vertical distance from the point where either trendline is broken. While the *ascending* and *descending* triangles have a built-in bias, the *symmetrical* triangle is inherently neutral. Since it is usually a continuation pattern, however, the symmetrical triangle does have forecasting value and implies that the prior trend will be resumed.

Flags and Pennants

These two short-term continuation patterns mark brief pauses, or resting periods, during dynamic market trends. Both are usually preceded by a steep price move (called the *pole*). In an uptrend, the steep advance pauses to catch its breath and moves sideways for two or three weeks. Then the uptrend continues on its way. The names aptly describe their appearance. The *pennant* is usually horizontal with two converging trendlines (like a small symmetrical triangle). The *flag* resembles a parallelogram that tends to slope against the trend. In an uptrend, therefore, the bull flag has a downward slope; in a downtrend, the bear flag slopes upward. Both patterns are said to "fly at half mast," meaning that they often occur near the middle of the trend, marking the halfway point in the market move. (See Figures 16 & 17.)

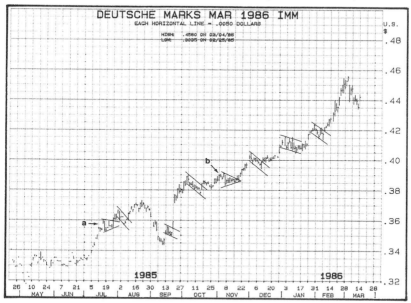

Figure 16: Examples of *flags* and *pennants*. Both patterns represent brief pauses in dynamic trends. Most of the patterns on this chart are *flags*, and resemble down-sloping parallelograms. *Flags* generally slope in the opposite direction of the prevailing trend. Two *pennants* are visible (Points a & b). *Pennants* are horizontal and have two converging trendlines. *Flags* and *pennants* rarely last longer than two or three weeks in an uptrend.

In addition to price patterns, there are several other formations that show up on the price charts and that provide the chartist with valuable insights. Among those formations are price gaps, key reversal days, and percentage retracements.

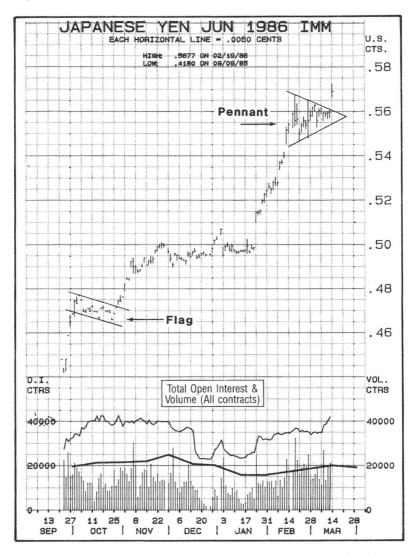

Figure 17: Examples of a bullish *flag* and *pennant*. The continuation pattern to the lower left is a bull *flag*. The pattern on the upper right is an excellent example of a *pennant* formation. The *pennant* resembles a small *symmetrical triangle*.

Chapter 6

PRICE GAPS

Gaps are simply areas on the bar chart where no trading has taken place. An upward gap occurs when the lowest price for one day is higher than the highest price of the preceding day. A downward gap means that the highest price for one day is lower than the lowest price of the preceding day. There are different types of gaps that appear at different stages of the trend. Being able to distinguish among them can provide useful and profitable market insights. Three types of gaps have forecasting value — breakaway, runaway and exhaustion gaps. (See Figure 18.)

The *breakaway* gap usually occurs on completion of an important price pattern and signals a significant market move. A breakout above the neckline of a head and shoulders bottom, for example, often occurs on a breakaway gap.

The *runaway* gap usually occurs after the trend is well underway. It often appears about halfway through the move (which is why it is also called a *measuring* gap since it gives some indication of how much of the move is left.) During uptrends, the breakaway and runaway gaps usually provide support below the market on subsequent market dips; during downtrends, these two gaps act as resistance over the market on bounces.

The *exhaustion* gap occurs right at the end of the market move and represents a last gasp in the trend. Sometimes an exhaustion gap is followed within a few days by a breakaway gap in the other direction, leaving several days of price action isolation by two gaps. This market phenomenon is called the *island reversal* and usually signals an important market turn.

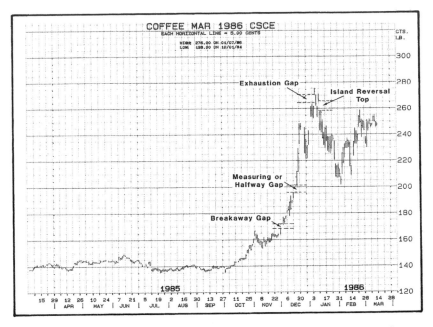

Figure 18: Examples of *gaps*. The *breakaway gap* launches the bull move. The measuring gap usually occurs at about the halfway point. The *exhaustion gap* occurs near the top. If prices gap downward after an *exhaustion gap* to the upside, an *island reversal top* is formed.

Chapter 7

THE KEY REVERSAL DAY

Another price formation is the *key reversal day*. This minor pattern often warns of an impending change in trend. In an uptrend, prices usually open higher, then break sharply to the downside and close below the previous day's closing price. (A bottom reversal day opens lower and closes higher.)

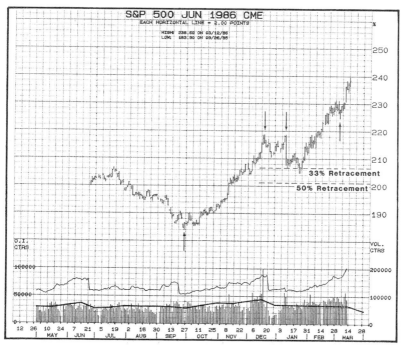

Figure 19: *Key reversal days* and *percentage retracements*. The arrows demonstrate the presence of *key reversal days*. These formations often signal important market turns, especially if they're accompanied by heavy volume. Corrections to the trend often retrace a third to a half before the trend is resumed. The downside correction in December and January retraced just beyond 33% of the prior uptrend, which is considered to be normal corrective action.

The wider the day's range and the heavier the volume, the more significant the warning becomes and the more authority it carries. *Outside* reversal days (where the high and low of the current day's range are both wider than the previous day's range) are considered more potent. The key reversal day is a relatively minor pattern taken on its own merits, but can assume major importance if other technical factors suggest that an important change in trend is eminent. (Figure 19.)

Chapter 8

PERCENTAGE RETRACEMENTS

Market trends seldom take place in straight lines. Most trend pictures show a series of zig-zags with several corrections against the existing trend. These corrections usually fall into certain predictable percentage parameters. The best-known example of this is the *fifty-percent retracement*. That is to say, a secondary, or intermediate, correction against a major uptrend often retraces about half of the prior uptrend before the bull trend is again resumed. Bear market bounces often recover about half of the prior downtrend.

A minimum retracement is usually about a *third* of the prior trend. The *two-thirds* point is considered the maximum retracement that is allowed if the prior trend is going to resume. A retracement beyond the two-thirds point usually warns of a trend reversal in progress.

Chapter 9

THE INTERPRETATION
OF VOLUME
AND OPEN INTEREST

Chartists employ a three-dimensional approach to market analysis that includes a study of price, volume, and open interest. Of the *three*, price is the most important. However, *volume* and *open interest* provide important secondary confirmation of the price action on the chart and often give advance warnings of an impending shift in trend. (See Figure 20.)

Volume is the number of futures contracts traded during a given time period, which is usually a day. It is similar to the number of common stock shares traded each day in the stock market. Open interest is the number of unliquidated or open contracts in a given futures market. Open interest is the total number of outstanding longs or shorts, but not the total of both. In other words, each futures contract consists of one long and one short position.

When used in conjunction with the price action, volume and open interest tell us something about the strength or weakness of the current price trend. Volume measures the pressure behind a given price move. As a rule, *heavier volume (marked by larger vertical bars at the bottom of the chart) should be present in the direction of the prevailing price trend*. During an uptrend, heavier volume should be seen during rallies, with lighter volume (smaller volume bars) during downside corrections. In downtrends, the heavier volume should occur on price selloffs. Bear market bounces should take place on a lighter volume.

Figure 20: The three-dimensional approach to chart analysis combines price, volume, and open interest. This lumber example paints a bullish picture. Price, volume, and open interest are all increasing together. Price measures the trend; heavy volume indicates strong upside pressure and confirms the upward trend in prices; rising open interest reflects new money flowing into the market, which is a necessary ingredient for a strong bull trend.

Volume is an Important Part of Price Patterns

Volume also plays an important role in the formation and resolution of price patterns. Each of the price patterns described previously has its own volume pattern. As a rule, volume tends to diminish as price patterns form. The subsequent breakout that resolves the pattern takes on added significance if the price breakout is accompanied by heavier volume. Heavier volume accompanying the breaking of trendlines and support or resistance levels lends greater weight to price activity.

Open Interest
Measures the Flow of Money

While volume measures the pressure or intensity behind the price move, open interest measures the flow of money. Each trade completed on the floor of a futures exchange has an impact on the open interest figure for that day. If both parties to the trade are initiating a new position (one long and one short), open interest increases by one contract. If both traders are liquidating an existing position (one selling an old long position and the other covering an old short position), open interest drops by one contract. If one of the traders is initiating a new position and the other offsetting an old position, there is no change in the open interest.

By monitoring the changes in the open interest figure at the end of the day, therefore, some conclusions can be drawn about the day's activity. Increasing open interest means that new money is flowing into the market. That increases the odds that the present trend will continue. Declining open interest suggests a liquidating market and implies that the price trend may be ending.

As a rule, rising prices and rising open interest are bullish (new buying); falling prices and rising open interest are bearish (aggressive short-selling); rising prices and falling open interest are bearish (long profit-taking and short-covering); falling prices and falling open interest are bullish (discouraged long liquidation). The following table combines the main points involved in price, volume and open interest analysis.

PRICE	VOLUME	OPEN INTEREST	INTERPRETATION
Rising	Rising	Rising	Market is strong
Rising	Falling	Falling	Market is weakening
Falling	Rising	Rising	Market is weak
Falling	Falling	Falling	Market is strengthening

Commitments of Traders Report

Another way to utilize open interest data is by monitoring the Commitments of Traders Reports. These statistics are released monthly by the Commodity Futures Trading Commission and are presented in tabular form in Bridge/CRB Futures Perspective immediately after the report is made public. As the accompanying table shows, the open interest figures at the end of the previous month are broken down into three categories — large hedgers, large speculators, and small traders. (See Figure 21.)

MARKETS	LARGE HEDGERS				LARGE SPECULATORS				SMALL TRADERS			
	Long	Short	Net	Δ	Long	Short	Net	Δ	Long	Short	Net	Δ
Cattle (Live)	17	40	-23	-4	8	5	+3	-3	73	54	+19	+6
Cocoa	85	66	+19	-5	2	17	-15	+1	12	16	-4	+4
Coffee	52	74	-22	+6	15	4	+11	-3	32	19	+13	-1
Copper	17	82	-65	-13	33	2	+31	+8	49	15	+34	+5
Corn	50	41	+9	-6	4	9	-5	+3	42	46	-4	+4
Cotton	23	55	-32	-2	13	6	+7	-2	61	36	+25	+4
Crude Oil (N.Y.)	60	62	-2	+6	16	17	-1	-8	18	16	+2	0
Gold (Comex)	65	49	+16	+3	7	9	-2	+1	20	35	-15	-6
Heating Oil #2	63	54	+9	0	5	17	-12	-4	29	27	+2	+2
Hogs	8	8	0	-5	17	7	+10	+11	69	78	-9	-5
Leaded Gas (N.Y.)	44	57	-13	+2	16	14	+2	+1	36	24	+12	-2
Lumber	14	50	-36	0	16	1	+15	-1	60	38	+22	+2
Orange Juice	34	69	-35	+7	9	2	+7	-5	54	25	+29	0
Platinum	14	65	-51	-7	25	8	+17	-2	60	25	+35	+10
Pork Bellies	6	17	11	-5	19	10	+3	+9	66	57	+9	-4
Silver (Comex)	35	55	-20	-2	11	13	-2	-1	44	22	+22	+3
Soybeans	32	52	-20	-19	14	5	+9	+10	48	36	+12	+9
Soybean Meal	45	59	-14	-2	13	3	+10	+1	40	35	+5	+2
Soybean Oil	50	47	+3	-21	8	6	+2	+11	39	42	-3	+13
Sugar "11"	35	84	-49	-14	18	1	+17	+15	47	14	+33	+1
Wheat (CHI)	33	19	+14	-7	6	20	-14	-1	53	54	-1	+7
Wheat (K.C.)	70	44	+26	-2	0	7	-7	+1	26	45	-19	+2
Wheat (Minn)	72	63	+9	-11	0	0	0	0	28	37	-9	+11
Euro $	60	62	-2	0	11	3	+8	+4	26	31	-5	2
T-Bills (90 Days)	32	81	-49	-5	24	2	+22	+10	44	17	+27	-5
T-Bonds	61	62	-1	+1	11	8	+3	-1	23	26	-3	-1
T-Notes	86	86	0	-7	6	5	+1	+5	6	7	-1	+2
NYSE Composite	22	40	-18	-15	29	35	-6	+25	43	19	+24	-10
S&P 500	41	61	-20	-22	12	5	+7	+8	48	34	+14	+15
Value Line	32	61	-29	+9	26	14	+12	+3	42	25	+17	-13
British Pound	25	61	-36	-20	41	17	+24	+15	33	22	+11	+4
Deutsche Mark	30	72	-42	-2	34	10	+24	+4	35	18	+17	-3
Japanese Yen	9	77	-68	-23	52	5	+47	+19	39	17	+22	+4
Swiss Franc	34	65	-31	-2	27	14	+13	+2	38	20	+18	+1

COMMITMENTS OF TRADERS—LARGE HEDGERS, SPECULATORS AND SMALL TRADERS
Open Interest Positions Shown in Percent (Rounded) as of March 31, 1986

Figure 21: The Commitments of Traders table. By monitoring these monthly statistics, the trader is able to determine what the three categories of traders are doing in the various markets.

The table shows not only the net positions for each group, but also the changes from the previous month. By monitoring the table, it is possible to draw some inferences concerning the relative bullish or bearish attitudes of the three respective groups. By monitoring the changes in the net figures from the previous month, shifts in those attitudes can also be spotted.

Research done by the Bridge Commodity Research Bureau over the years suggests that, of the three groups, the large hedgers have the most impressive track record in calling market turns. Large traders have also done well historically. Small traders have generally been the least successful. By studying the Commitments of Traders Report each month, the futures trader is able to study the changing bullish and bearish attitudes of the three groups. Armed with this valuable information, the trader can gain more insight into what the more successful traders are doing and those not so successful. The purpose of the exercise is, of course, to align one's position with the more successful participants.

Seasonal Considerations in Open Interest

While the numbers presented in the Commitments of Traders table provide useful information on the character of bullish or bearish market sponsorship, it should be recognized that there are *seasonal* movements in the shifting open interest alignment among the three groups which should also be taken into consideration when interpreting the numbers. On a more general level, it should also be pointed out that open interest numbers plotted on the daily bar chart have their own seasonal tendencies. The dashed line near the bottom of the bar chart, showing the 6-year average of the open interest numbers, represents the seasonal tendency for those years. The actual (solid) open interest line takes on more significance when it deviates from the seasonal norm.

Chapter 10

OBTAINING VALUABLE LONG-TERM PERSPECTIVE WITH WEEKLY AND MONTHLY CONTINUATION CHARTS

Bar chart analysis is not limited to daily bar charts. In addition to the daily bar charts that are provided each week, *Bridge/CRB Futures Perspective* makes available to its subscriber's long-term weekly and monthly continuation charts.

These weekly and monthly charts provide a valuable long-term perspective on market history that cannot be obtained by using daily charts alone. The daily bar chart usually shows up to ten months of price history for each futures contract. Weekly continuation charts show almost five years of data, while the monthly charts go back over 20 years. (Figures 22 & 23)

By studying these charts, the chartist gets a better idea of long-term trends, where historic support and resistance levels are located, and is able to obtain a clearer perspective on the more recent action revealed in the daily charts. These weekly and monthly charts lend themselves quite well to standard chart analysis described in the preceding pages. The view held by some market observers that chart analysis is useful only for short-term analysis and timing is simply not true. The principles of chart analysis can be used in any time dimension.

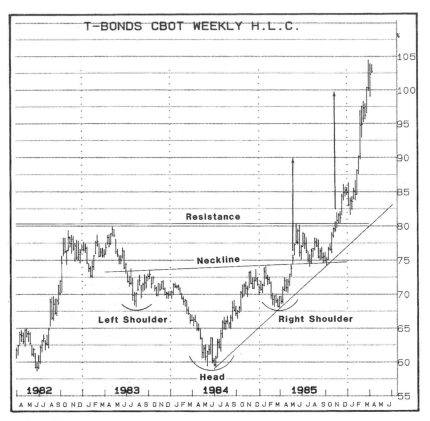

Figure 22: A demonstration of the long-term perspective achieved with weekly continuation charts. A major *head and shoulders* bottom (spanning 3 years) was completed in early 1985 on the upside penetration of the *neckline*. An upside objective was measured to 90-00. By measuring the entire base (from 60-00 to 80-00), an even higher target to 100-00 was given. Notice the major *up trendline* from the summer of 1984 that contained the selloff in late 1985 near 75-00.

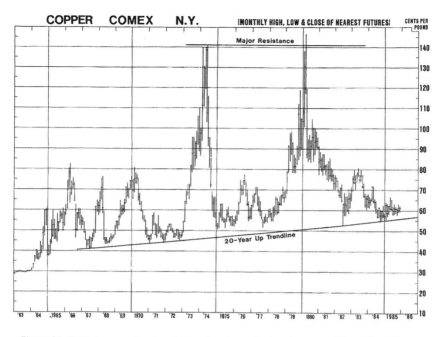

Figure 23: Historic *support* and *resistance* levels can be found on a monthly continuation chart. The 1980 top near 140 coincided with the 1974 top. Notice that the bear market low in 1982 and again in 1984 held above a 20-year *up trendline*. These long-term charts lend themselves quite well to standard chart analysis and provide a valuable long-term perspective.

How to Construct Continuation Charts

Since commodity futures contracts expire and have a limited life span, the construction of long-term charts presents some problems. There are various ways to construct weekly and monthly charts to provide the necessary continuity in the price history. The technique used by Bridge Commodity Research Bureau is simply to link the prices of the nearest expiring contracts. That is to say, the price of the nearest delivery month is always used.

Some chartists use more complicated methods of chart construction to smooth out the transition from one *spot* to the other. However, since these continuation charts are used mainly for long-term analysis, it is doubtful that the more complex methods of chart construction provide much of an advantage. The technique of construction utilized in *Bridge/CRB Futures Perspective* has the benefit of simplicity and, more importantly, has proven to be quite effective over the years.

Going From the Long Term to the Short Term

As indispensable as the daily bar charts are to market timing and analysis, a thorough chart analysis should begin with the monthly and weekly charts — and in that order. The purpose of that approach is to provide the analyst with the necessary long-term view as a starting point. Once that is obtained on the 20-year monthly chart, the 5-year weekly chart should be consulted. Only then should the daily chart be studied. In other words, the proper order to follow is to begin with a solid overview and then gradually shorten the time horizon. (For even more microscopic market analysis, the study of the daily chart can be followed by the scrutiny of intraday charts.)

These long-term charts become especially valuable when individual futures contracts move into new contract highs or lows. The chartist following only the daily chart finds him or herself in unknown territory with no way to determine future support or resistance levels and possible price targets. By consulting the continuation charts, historic support and resistance levels can be identified and then used as an effective method of determining possible future price objectives.

Chapter 11

THE BRIDGE/CRB FUTURES PRICE INDEX
AND THE BRIDGE/CRB FUTURES GROUP INDICES

The practice of beginning one's analysis with the broader view and gradually narrowing one's focus has another important application in the utilization of the various Bridge/CRB indices. Before analyzing any individual commodity market, it's necessary first to determine the general environment influencing all commodity prices, and then to examine the behavior of the group that contains the market under consideration.

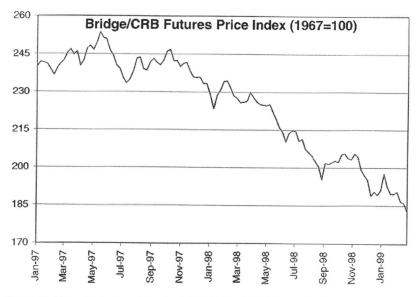

Figure 24: The solid line is a daily chart of the Bridge/CRB Futures Price Index of 17 non-financial commodity markets (see box). It should be the starting point in the analysis of any individual market. The Index tells the trader whether commodity prices in general are in a bullish or bearish environment.

Bridge/CRB Futures Perspective includes short-term and long-term charts on the Bridge/CRB Futures Price Index. The Bridge/CRB Futures Price Index is an unweighted geometric average of 17 active (non-financial) futures markets, using a base year of 1967 (1967=100). Created in 1957, The Bridge/CRB Index has become the industry standard for measuring the rise or fall in the general commodity price level.

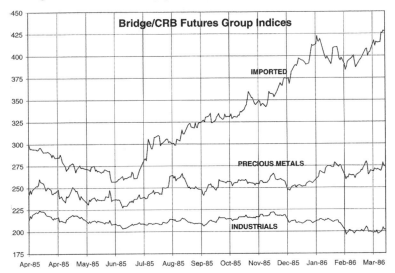

Figure 25a: The second step in the analytical process is to study the various group indices. In this example, the Imported group looks bullish. The Industrials have been in a downward, but are stabilizing. Take note of the fact that the Precious Metals Index appears to be forming a bullish "ascending triangle."

The Bridge/CRB Index
Should be the First Step in Market Analysis

Since commodity markets tend to move in the same direction (much like common stocks), the first step in any individual market analysis is to determine which way the general commodity price level is moving. The Bridge/CRB Futures Price Index is ideal for that purpose. (See Figure 24.)

As an illustration of this point, consider that the 1970s saw a rising Bridge/CRB Index reflecting strong inflationary pressures. Individual commodity markets were carried along in a generally bullish market environment. The inflationary bubble burst at the end of 1980, when the Bridge/CRB Index began a 5-year descent. Those five years witnessed a generally bearish environment in commodity markets, dominated by disinflationary pressures and falling commodity prices. Knowledge of which way the Bridge/CRB Index was moving during both periods of time could have had a decisive influence on a trader's assessment of the various commodity groups and individual commodity markets. *An analysis of the Bridge/CRB Futures Price Index should be the starting point of all commodity market analysis.*

The Second Step:
The Bridge/CRB Futures Group Indices

Having determined the climate affecting the overall commodity price level, the second step in the process is to monitor the six Bridge/CRB futures group indices. (Figure 25 a & b.) The group indices allow the trader to determine the relative strength or weakness among the various market sectors. As an illustration, if the composite Bridge/CRB Index is turning higher and the trader is seeking a profitable buying situation, he or she would seek out the market group with the strongest chart pattern. Having accomplished that, two-thirds of the search would be complete.

One final step remains, however.

ENERGY	GRAINS	INDUSTRIALS
Crude Oil Heating Oil Natural Gas	Corn Soybeans Wheat	Cotton Copper
LIVESTOCK	**PRECIOUS METALS**	**SOFTS**
Lean Hogs Live Cattle	Gold Platinum Silver	Cocoa Coffee FCOJ Sugar

Figure 25b: Bridge/CRB Futures Group Indices and Components

The Third Step:
The Individual Markets

The third and final task would be to consult the charts of the individual markets. By this time, the trader has already determined whether commodity prices are rising or falling, what the various group indices are doing, and is ready to zero in on the individual markets.

Suppose that a trader has decided to buy gold. He or she would first determine whether the Bridge/CRB Index is rising or falling. If it were rising, that would have a bullish influence on all commodity markets. The Bridge/CRB Precious Metals Index would then be studied, since that's the group containing the gold market. If the group index were also turning higher, the prospective gold bull would then proceed into a study of the gold charts themselves. Two-thirds of the work would already have been done before arriving at a study of the market under scrutiny.

The correct analytical procedure takes three steps, in the order suggested above. Some commodity traders begin their analysis of the individual markets, ignoring the valuable information provided by the Bridge/CRB indices. That's like making a decision on the direction of a common stock without considering the direction of the broad stock market averages or the industry group of which the individual stock is a part.

Technical analysis of the Bridge/CRB Futures Price Index and the Bridge/CRB futures group indices should begin with the monthly and weekly charts to provide the necessary long-term perspective in the fashion described in the previous section. These broader indices lend themselves quite well to standard chart analysis.

Chapter 12

MOVING AVERAGES AND OSCILLATORS

In the realm of technical indicators, *moving averages* and *oscillators* are extremely popular with futures technicians and with good reason. Moving averages smooth the price action and make it easier to spot the underlying trends. Precise trend signals can be obtained from the interaction between a price and an average or between two or more averages themselves. Since the moving average is constructed by averaging several days' closing prices, however, it tends to lag behind the price action. The shorter the average (meaning the fewer days used in its calculation), the more sensitive it is to price changes and the closer it trails the price action. A longer average (with more days included in its calculation) tracks the price action from a greater distance and is less responsive to trend changes. The moving average is easily quantified and lends itself especially well to historical testing. Mainly for those reasons, it is the mainstay of most mechanical trend-following systems.

Oscillators are used to identify *overbought* and *oversold* market conditions. The oscillator is plotted on the bottom of the price chart and fluctuates within a horizontal band. When the oscillator line reaches the upper limit of the band, a market is said to be overbought and vulnerable to a short-term setback. When the line is at the bottom of the range, the market is oversold and probably due for a rally. The oscillator helps to measure market extremes and tells the chartist when a market advance or decline has become over-extended.

Moving Averages

There is no limit to the combination of moving averages that may be used when analyzing market movements. Bridge/CRB traditionally has used a combination of 10- and 40-day moving averages in its analysis. The 10-day average is a simple addition of the preceding 10 days' closing prices divided by 10. The 40-day average is a weighted combination of 10-, 20-, and 40-day moving averages. While a simple average gives equal weight to each day's price, a weighted average places increased importance on the more recent price activity.

When two moving averages are employed, trend signals can be given in two ways. One is by the crossing of the two averages. When the shorter (10-day) average crosses above the longer (40-day), an uptrend signal is given. When the 10-day crosses below the 40-, a downtrend signal is given. A trend signal can also be generated when the closing price crosses the 40-day average. A close over the 40-day average initiates an uptrend; a close below the 40-day average signals a downtrend. Since market trends tend to remain in motion, these trend signals often stay in effect for several weeks or even months.

Chapter 13

COMPUTER TREND ANALYSIS

Chart analysis tends to be very subjective. Computer signals, however, are very precise and not subject to interpretation. Many futures traders base their trading strategies exclusively on mechanical technical systems. Others use mechanical signals merely as a confirmation of conclusions arrived at by more traditional chart analysis. The first rule of successful trading is *to trade in the direction of the trend.* Trend direction, however, isn't always crystal clear. By utilizing computer trend signals, the chartist has a more objective yardstick to ensure that he or she is not bucking an established trend.

The Electronic Futures Trend Analyzer (EFTA)

Twenty years ago, the Commodity Research Bureau developed a computerized trading system for the purpose of removing the emotional human element from market forecasting. Since then, countless trading programs, timing theories, and sure-fire techniques have been designed and popularized by an even wider universe of individuals and companies for the purpose of predicting the trends in the futures markets.

The EFTA system analyzes four different technical studies to categorize markets as trending up, sideways, or down. These four studies are a combination of moving averages, price volatility, market momentum, and various time cycles. Support and resistance levels are recalculated daily and serve as "stops" when the market is in a trend phase, and mark the breakout levels for new up or down trends when markets are in a sideways congestion area.

The EFTA model was created to identify medium to long-term trends and is designed to maintain positions through minor corrections. In recent years, the currency, interest rate, energy, and soft commodity markets have provided some of the best returns due to sustained trends in their component markets. One, five, and ten-year performance studies are available from Bridge/CRB upon request.

In the uncertain world of futures trading, EFTA will insure participation in major trends whenever and wherever they occur. The universe of markets EFTA analyzes is diverse and covers all major U.S. futures. (See figure 26.)

NOTE: It is not the intent of Bridge/CRB to represent the Electronic Futures Trend Analyzer solely as a trading system, but equally as an important and demonstrably valuable check on other methods of price analysis that may depend too heavily upon human evaluations. Its greatest advantage lies in its purely mathematical approach, which rules out emotionalism, a serious liability in the world of futures trading.

Using the Electronic Futures Trend Analyzer as a Technical Filter and as a Mechanical Alert for Possible Trend Changes

The column headings in the table are self-explanatory except for support and resistance. Those numbers mark price levels where changes in trend would occur. A closing price beyond those support and resistance levels would produce the following trend changes:

> From *up* to *sideways* on a close below support.
> From *down* to *sideways* on a close over resistance.
> From *sideways* to *up* on a close over resistance and from *sideways* to *down* on a close under support.

Support and resistance levels listed in the table can be inserted right on the price charts themselves, so that the analyst knows in advance where computer trend changes will occur. Computer signals can then be incorporated right into the chartist's own analysis and can become another valuable technical indicator. Fundamentally oriented traders, who or not as adept at the skill of charting, can use these computer signals as a filter on their own trading decisions.

COMPUTER TREND ANALYZER

Commodity	Delivery	Computer Trend	Trend Started		Current Computer		Market Close 4/11/86	Week's Change
			Date	Price	Support	Resistance		
BRITISH POUND	JUNE '86	UP	2/19/86	1.4335	1.4430		1.4735	+ $.0345
CATTLE (Live)	JUNE '86	DOWN	3/7/86	58.80		58.35	56.92	+ 2.90¢
COCOA	MAY '86	DOWN	3/24/86	1892		1950	1801	– $28
COFFEE "C"	MAY '86	SIDEWAYS	2/24/86	256.01	221.30	259.20	232.23	+ 9.00¢
COPPER	MAY '86	DOWN	4/3/86	64.15		66.85	64.65	+ .50¢
CORN	MAY '86	DOWN FROM SIDE	4/9/86	228 1/4		237	227 3/4	– 5 3/4¢
COTTON #2	MAY '86	DOWN FROM SIDE	4/7/86	61.90		64.65	61.96	– 1.49¢
CRUDE OIL	JUNE '86	SIDEWAYS	4/4/86	12.87	12.00	14.00	13.46	+ $.59
DEUTSCHE MARK	JUNE '86	DOWN	3/25/86	.4293		.4410	.4345	+ $.0142
EURODOLLAR	JUNE '86	UP	2/14/86	92.11	93.06		93.33	+ .20%
GAS (Leaded)	JUNE '86	UP FROM SIDE	4/7/86	44.10	38.05		44.68	+ 3.58¢
GAS (Unleaded)	JUNE '86	UP FROM SIDE	4/7/86	43.80	37.80		44.70	+ 3.90¢
GOLD (Comex)	JUNE '86	DOWN	4/1/86	337.00		352.50	347.50	+ $9.10
HEATING OIL#2	JUNE '86	DOWN	3/13/86	39.54		41.90	40.06	+ 1.89¢
HOGS	JUNE '86	DOWN	4/4/86	41.15		44.45	42.42	+ 1.27¢
JAPANESE YEN	JUNE '86	DOWN FROM SIDE	4/7/86	.5492		.5675	.5628	+ $.0063
LUMBER	MAY '86	UP	2/19/86	153.10	181.00		184.30	– $.40
MMI – MAXI	JUNE '86	SIDE FROM UP	4/7/86	323.00	320.65	338.50	332.45	+ 8.15%
MUNI-BONDS	JUNE '86	SIDE FROM UP	4/11/86	97–03	96–15	101–17	97–03	– 1 9/32
NYSE (NYFE)	JUNE '86	SIDEWAYS	4/3/86	134.10	132.40	137.60	136.55	+ 4.35%
ORANGE JUICE	MAY '86	UP	3/25/86	93.95	88.65		93.10	– 1.40¢
PLATINUM	JULY '86	UP FROM SIDE	4/7/86	425.00	401.00		437.80	+ $27.80
PORK BELLIES	MAY '86	DOWN	4/3/86	54.20		58.70	52.30	+ .10¢
SILVER (N.Y.)	MAY '86	SIDE FROM DOWN	4/11/86	556.00	531.25	572.85	556.00	+ 33.50
SOYBEANS	MAY '86	DOWN	4/4/86	523		536	524 1/2	+ 1 1/2¢
SOYBEAN MEAL	MAY '86	DOWN	3/31/86	153.70		158.30	155.30	+ $2.50
SOYBEAN OIL	MAY '86	SIDE FROM UP	4/9/86	17.41	17.35	18.70	17.43	– .54¢
S&P 500	JUNE '86	SIDEWAYS	4/3/86	232.75	229.25	238.45	236.65	+ 7.75%
SUGAR "11"	OCT. '86	SIDE FROM UP	4/11/86	8.30	7.65	8.90	8.30	– .63¢
SWISS FRANC	JUNE '86	DOWN	3/25/86	.5120		.5265	.5205	+ $.0153
T-BILLS (IMM)	JUNE '86	UP	2/4/86	93.20	94.10		94.42	+ .22%
T-BONDS (CBoT)	JUNE '86	UP	2/3/86	84–27	100–07		102–13	+ 2 2/32
T-NOTES (CBoT)	JUNE '86	UP	2/3/86	92–22	101–25		103	+ 1 7/32
VALUE LINE (K.C.)	JUNE'86	DOWN	4/10/86	232.10		240.00	238.60	+ 6.50%
WHEAT (Chi)	MAY '86	DOWN FROM UP	4/10/86	286 3/4		306	286 1/4	– 24 1/4¢

#TREND CHANGES ##TREND REVERSALS *CONTRACT TRANSFERS

Figure 26: The Electronic Futures Trend Analyzer, as published by Bridge/CRB. These mechanical signals can be used independently or incorporated into the chartist's analysis.

The notation # in column one identifies those markets where trend changes have occurred over the past week. The notation ## identifies those contracts where trend reversals have taken place. That valuable information can be the starting point in the search for profitable trading ideas. The trader is immediately alerted to those situations where a trend change has occurred. He or she can then examine those situations more closely. The Electronic Futures Trend Analyzer is a flexible technical tool that enables the trader to blend the computer's objectivity with his or her own subjective analysis.

Chapter 14

COMMODITY SPREADS AND RATIOS

Commodity *spreads* (also called *straddles*) measure the price difference between two futures contracts. When initiating a spread, a trader simultaneously buys one contract (goes long) and sells another one short. Instead of profiting from *absolute* price changes, the spread trader hopes to benefit from the widening or the narrowing of the spread *differential*. Spreads can be made between two contracts in the same commodity (interdelivery), between two different but related commodities (intercommodity), or between commodities on different exchanges (intermarket). Commodity *ratios*, by contrast, *divide* one price entity by another. (For example, the widely followed gold/silver ratio.)

By monitoring the *relative strength* between different markets, the trader is better able to select from among several possible trading opportunities. As a rule, a trader looking for a buying opportunity would concentrate his or her capital in the strongest markets. A short seller would be looking for the weakest contracts in the weakest markets.

The relationship between different delivery months in the same market often provides valuable information about that market's strength or weakness. The nearby months often lead a market move, either up or down. "Bull spreading" involves buying a nearby month and selling a deferred. A "bear spreader" would sell the nearby and buy the deferred. By monitoring these relationships, the market analyst can also get advanced warnings of a change in market trend.

Technical analysis can be applied to spread and ratio charts. Trendlines and moving averages, for example, can help measure trends on spreads and ratios and can alert the user to changes in those trends. Whether or not the chartist is interested in spread trading per se, a close monitoring of the spread and ratio charts can add a valuable dimension to market analysis.

Chapter 15

COMMODITY OPTIONS

Commodity options give the holder the right, but not the obligation, to purchase (in the case of a *call*) or sell (in the case of a *put*) an underlying futures contract at a specific price within a specified period of time. In its simplest application, a trader who is bullish on a futures market can simply purchase a *call*; a trader who is bearish can simply purchase a *put*.

Options trading is another way to take advantage of the unusually high leverage and profit potential in the futures markets. The main advantage in options trading is *limited risk*. The option trader pays a *premium* to purchase the option. If the market doesn't move as expected, the option simply expires. The maximum loss the option trader can suffer is the size of the premium.

There are countless option strategies that can be utilized by option traders. However, most option strategies require a market view. In other words, the option trader must first determine whether the market price of the underlying futures contract is going to rise, fall, or stay relatively flat. This is because the major factor influencing the value of an option is the performance of its underlying futures contract. In determining an appropriate option strategy, its important to remember that *the principles of market analysis are not applied to the option itself, but to the underlying futures contract.*

Therefore, it can be seen that the principles of chart analysis covered in the preceding pages and their application to the futures markets play an important role in commodity options trading. It also follows that the charts of the underlying futures contracts published in *Bridge/CRB Futures Perspective* are essential working tools in the development of successful option strategies.

Chapter 16

THE PRINCIPLE
OF CONFIRMATION

The principle of confirmation holds that the more technical evidence supporting a given analysis, the stronger the conclusion becomes. In the study of an individual market, for example, all of the delivery months should be pointing in the same direction. If some contracts are pointing up and the others down, be suspicious. Consult other markets in the same group. A bullish analysis in gold would be less than convincing if the other precious metals (silver and platinum) were trending lower. Since markets in the same group tend to move together, make sure that the other markets agree with the group being studied. Be sure to check the Bridge/CRB Futures Price Index to see which way commodity prices in general are moving.

Look at the various technical indicators to see if they agree. Are the chart patterns being confirmed by the volume and open interest? Do the moving averages and oscillators confirm the chart analysis? Which way is the computer trend moving? What do the weekly and monthly continuation charts show? While it is seldom that all of these technical factors will point in the same direction, it pays to have as many of them in your corner as possible.

Chapter 17

SUMMARY AND CONCLUSION

We have provided here an introduction to technical analysis as it is applied to the futures markets. We've discussed briefly the major tools utilized by the futures chartist, including: basic chart analysis, the study of volume and open interest, moving averages and oscillators, computer trend signals, spreads and ratios, weekly and monthly continuation charts, and the Bridge/CRB indices. The successful futures trader learns how to combine all these elements into one coherent theory of market analysis. By including many of the essential tools of the trade, each issue of *Bridge/CRB Futures Perspective* makes that task a good deal easier.

The many software and internct based products available on the market today also provide powerful tools that make charting and technical analysis much easier — and far more accessible to general investors — than ever before. The CD-rom demo disk included with this book contains a full suite of technical analysis tools that allow you to create charts easily, have instant access to historical data, and the ability to create, backtest and optimize self designed trading systems without any programming knowledge or experience.

▲　▲　▲　▲　▲

Technical analysis provides an excellent vehicle for *market forecasting*, either with or without fundamental input. Where technical analysis becomes absolutely essential, however, is in the area of *market timing*. Since the futures markets are so highly leveraged, relatively small market moves tend to have a greater impact on a trader's equity. Market timing is purely technical in nature, so successful participation in the futures markets dictates some application of technical analysis.

It's not necessary to be an expert chartist to benefit from chart analysis. However, chart analysis will go a long way in keeping the trader on the right side of the market and in helping to pinpoint market entry and exit points, which are so vital to trading success. Whether the futures participant is a speculator, a hedger, a spread or an option trader, it's to his or her advantage to learn about chart analysis.

Recommended Reading

This booklet does not include discussion of the finer points of chart analysis or the more advanced aspects of technical theory such as point and figure charting, time cycles, Elliott Wave Theory, the methods of W.D. Gann, and the broader range of computerized technical systems and indicators. For a much more definitive treatment of the subject, it is suggested that the reader consult the "bible" of future's market technicians, Mr. Murphy's, *Technical Analysis of the Financial Markets: A Comprehensive Guide to Trading Methods and Applications* - and other books listed in the resource guide that follows.

Trading
Resource
Guide

▲ ▲ ▲ ▲ ▲

TOOLS FOR SUCCESS
IN TRADING

Martin Pring's Introduction to Technical Analysis
A CD-Rom Seminar and Workbook

by Martin J. Pring

The foremost expert on technical analysis and forecasting financial markets gives you a one-on-one course in every aspect of technical analysis. This interactive guide explains how to evaluate trends, highs & lows, price/volume relationships, price patterns, moving averages, and momentum indicators.

The accompanying CD-ROM includes videos, animated diagrams, audio clips and interactive tests. It's the user-friendly way to master technical analysis from an industry icon.

304 pp $49.95 Item # 8521

Analyzing Bar Charts for Profit

by John Magee

A straightforward guide teaching the time-tested approach of using technical analysis to minimize risk and boost profits. From the bar chart "king" you'll learn: Classical chart patterns; How to identify trends and trading ranges; Tops, bottoms and what they mean to your bottom line. Plus, the "Magee Method" of buying/selling. "It's the best explanation of the technical process ever written."

224 pp $39.95 Item #2318

Point & Figure Charting

by Thomas J. Dorsey.
Here's the first new work on Point & Figure in 30 years. Today's leading expert shows how to use point & figure to chart price movements on stocks, options, futures and mutual funds. Learn to interpret the point and figure charts and recognize patterns that signal outstanding opportunities. Also covers how to combine point and figure with technical analysis for unbeatable success. You can't afford to pass by this valuable trading tool, and Dorsey makes it easier than ever.
304 pp $59.95 Item #2364

Candlestick Charting Explained

by Gregory Morris
Brand new book on this phenomenal indicator takes the guesswork out of candlestick analysis. Go beyond the basic theory to build a thorough system using the latest in computer analysis techniques and to identify trends, patterns, tops, bottoms — and more. $35.00 Item #2347

Technical Analysis of the Financial Markets

by John Murphy
From how to read charts to understanding indicators and the crucial role of technical analysis in investing, you won't find a more thorough or up-to-date source. Revised and expanded for today's changing financial world, it applies to equities as well as the futures markets.
$70.00 Item #10239

The New CRB Commodity Yearbook
by Bridge

It's the reference "Bible" researchers and commodity traders must have. Newly update, fact-filled and comprehensive, it combines information unavailable in any other single source including: current charts, tables, and graphs on over 100 commodities supplemented with articles on trading techniques and strategies by top industry experts. $99.95 Item #6039

Handbook of Technical Analysis:
A Comprehensive Guide to Analytical Methods, Trading Systems and Technical Indicators

by Darrell Jobman, $55.00
In-depth look at all aspects of technical analysis. The roster of contributors is a "Who's Who" of trading: Wilder on RSI, Schwager on uses and abuses of technical analysis, Pring on momentum, Prechter on Elliott Wave and more. From bar charts to candlesticks, volume to Gann — it's a #1 guide to the profit-grabbing techniques of the masters. Item #3419

New Market Wizards

by Jack Schwager
Meet a new generation of market killers. These hot traders make millions — often in hours — and consistently outperform peers. They use vastly different methods, but share big successes. Now, you can meet them and learn their methods. How do they do it? How can you do it? Learn their winning ways with this bestseller. 493 pp $39.95 Item #2106

The Art of Short Selling

by Kathryn F. Staley
Finally, a book showing how to cash in on this lucrative yet overlooked strategy. Staley explains what it is, how it works, best type of companies to short and never before released methods of the world's top short sellers. There's no better time to position yourself to profit from any stock sell off.
288 pp $49.95 Item #2006

Pattern, Price & Time
Using Gann Theory in Trading Systems

by James Herczyk
Here's the first book to simplify Gann's breakthrough techniques for beating the markets. Also shows how to integrate Gann theory into modern computer charting methods.
$59.95 Item #8438

Profits in Volume: Equivolume Charting

by Richard W. Arms, Jr.
This method places emphasis on trading range and volume-considered the two primary factors in technical analysis. They give an accurate appraisal of the supply/demand factors that influence a stock. With this critical factor you can determine if a stock is moving with ease or difficulty and - thereby - make more on-target investing decisions.
$39.95 Item #6780

To order any book listed and get a special 15%

"Trade Secrets" discount

Call 1-800-272-2855 ext. T176

CRB Futures Perspective

Don't miss out on trades because you don't have the big picture! Get a wealth of information on 87 international markets, from Bridge/CRB's premier chart publication. See the difference 42 years of experience makes. Every oversized 10" x 12" weekly chart book presents pages of daily and weekly bar charts, technical analysis studies, weekly market commentaries, the CFTC Commitment of Traders Report and so much more:

• At-a-Glance Analysis:
No More flipping back & forth between pages because an entire market is charted on facing pages. Easy-to-update gridlines, multiple contracts and studies also assist your analysis.

• Info Tailored to Your Trading Needs:
Choose from 3 editions — so you get only the information you want and need. Select the...

> **Financial Edition,** which covers 58 global financial markets. Reg. 3 month rate: $110
> Trade Secrets rate: $90 Item #7115

> **The Agricultural Edition,** covering 40 global agricultural markets.   Reg. 3 month rate: $100
> Trade Secrets rate: $79 Item #7116

> **The Full Edition,** which includes both Agricultural and Financial Editions. Reg. 3 month rate: $185
> Trade Secrets rate: $150 Item #7114

To order any book listed and get a special 15% "Trade Secrets" discount Call 1-800-272-2855 ext. T176

CRB Wall Charts & Desk Sets

Issued each April and October, this unique desk set combo offers 10-year weekly & 20-year monthly charts, allowing you to take a long, historical look at any of 30 markets. Contract specifications and historic highs and lows are included for each market. Put historical trends at your fingertips with this desk set.
$69.95 Item #7117

Traders' Library Bookstore - www.traderslibrary.com,
the #1 source for trading and investment books, videos and related products.

Bridge Financial - www.crbindex.com, a comprehensive
source of products and services for futures and options traders. This "one-stop" site offers current quotes, on-line data, books, software products, news and information - from one of the world's leading financial information source.

MurphyMorris - www.murphymorris.com, The site of
Technical Analysis gurus John Murphy and Greg Morris. A perfect site for both beginners and those more experienced in Technical Analysis.

Wall Street Directory - www.wsdinc.com, the best
directory of financial sites on the web. A comprehensive source that will help you find the answers to all your financial questions, and point you in the right direction.

Dorsey Wright - www.dorseywright.com,
The top source for information on Point & Figure analysis and comprehensive Point & Figure charts.

Equity Analytics - www.e-analytics.com, An excellent
educational resource with extensive glossaries for technical analysis and many other topics.

FutureSource — www.futuresource.com, a comprehensive source of information for futures and other traders providing futures quotes, settlement prices, charts, FWN news, chat rooms and other useful tools for traders of all levels.

Futures Magazine - www.futuresmag.com, filled with information for futures and options traders, plus books, videos and dates of their popular trading conferences.

Omega Research - www.omegresearch.com, information on Omega products, support and solution providers. Also find a listing of their free trading seminars.

Track Data - www.tdc.com, a supplier of electronically delivered financial data since 1981 - with several services specifically designed to assist day traders. Timely market data, financial data bases, historical information, data manipulation tools and analytical services are available.

Bloomberg - www.bloomberg.com, This major financial web site has it all: news, quotes, hot market information, lifestyle updates, investing tools and resources, research — and more. Turn to the industry leader for all your financial needs.

Telerate TAG conference From Bridge For over 20 years,

TAG (Technical Analysis Group) has presented annually 3-days of balanced workshops for new and experienced traders alike. Structured to give you a firm foundation and keep you abreast of the latest research and techniques, TAG helps you further your technical analysis education in a structured environment designed to teach. Learn to trade with confidence and get hands-on instruction from the industry's top traders.
For information contact: Tim Slater, 504-592-4550

Futures West & South

Twice yearly, Futures Magazine Group presents 3-day conferences featuring in-depth presentations by trading experts, plus an exhibit hall showcasing the newest products and services for traders. You'll find everything related to trading in an intimate, hands-on setting that allows you to mingle with the experts. With tracks for beginning, intermediate and advanced trading - something is offered for every active trader.
For information contact: Russ Koehler, conference director
800-221-4352 or 312/977-0999

Omega World

The growing trend toward system trading is clear and OmegaWorld is the premier conference dedicated to system trading and development. Those willing to take more control of their investment program will find of wealth of information, along with workshops geared towards beginning and advanced attendees. Serious, in-depth sessions, exhibits of the industry's top products and latest software and lots of exciting events make this a stand-out event for all traders.
For information contact: 800-327-3794

MurphyMorris, Inc.

Technical Analysis Tools from the World's Foremost Market Technician

John Murphy Explains Market Analysis
Volume 1 - Visual Analysis CD-rom Version
Item #10151 $49.95

Almost an hour of easy-to-follow video animation with John Murphy explaining the basic concepts of visual analysis. John walks you through Charts, Trends, Moving Averages, Chart Patterns, Sector Analysis - and more. Gain insight into John's personal techniques. Learn "Murphy's Laws" from a full motion video of John using state-of-the-art graphics that make this an easy way to learn basic to complex concepts - from a top technician.

> Requirements: Windows operating system, 486 or higher, CD-rom drive (sound card recommended).

Both for $75
Item #10562

The Visual Investor
How to Spot Market Trends
John Murphy $39.95 Item #2379

> **Software Disk Included!**

This book is the perfect companion to Murphy's CD-rom. *The Visual Investor* tracks the ups and downs of stock prices by visually comparing charts - instead of relying on complex formulas and technical concepts. Introduces readers to Intermarket Analysis - a proven analytical approach based on evaluating the impact different markets have on each other. Includes software deme disks, step-by-step instructions for using charts and graphs, and more - from CNBC's resident technical analyst for over 6 years.

Order NOW: 800-272-2855 ext. T176
Email orders to: tee@traderslibrary.com
- reference code T176 and save over 15%!

About the Author

▲ ▲ ▲ ▲ ▲

John Murphy has authored three best-selling books on technical analysis, including "Intermarket Technical Analysis" and "The Visual Investor." His latest work, "Technical Analysis of the Financial Markets," (1999) is a revised edition of his 1986 classic text which has been translated into eight languages. He is president of MURPHYMORRIS.COM which produces interactive educational products on technical analysis and online analysis for investors. As the former host of CNBC's *Tech Talk* show and a speaker at all the major trading and investment forums and conferences around the world, Mr. Murphy is one of the most recognized and highly respected technical analysts of our time.

Notes

Notes

About the CD-rom Disk Included:

Technical Analysis has become the trader's tool to market profits. With increased use of PC's and the internet, the ability to chart markets is easier and more affordable than ever. Now, this **free demo disk** puts technical analysis implementation *right at your fingertips*.

This disk includes:

1 A full working version of **CRB PowerLink**, an Internet Interface to downloading historical data from Bridge/CRB over the Internet.

2 The full **CRB/SystemMaker software** program. This is a full technical analysis application that creates all of the usual charts and technical studies. But its real attraction is its ability to create, backtest, and optimize self designed trading systems without any programming knowledge or experience.

3 A demonstration of the **"CRB Yearbooks on CD-ROM"** product. This product contains the full content, including all text tables, and charts, from every CRB Yearbook published since 1965.

To enable the free two-week free data trial, and the historical data to run CRB SystemMaker, call 800-621-5271 to set up your password.
Outside the U.S. call 312-454-1801.